first book of
cars

Isabel Thomas

For Harry, Joey and Oscar

Published 2013 by
A&C Black
An imprint of Bloomsbury Publishing Plc
50 Bedford Square, London, WC1B 3DP

www.bloomsbury.com

ISBN 978-1-4081-9225-2

A CIP catalogue for this book is available from the British Library.

This book is produced using paper that is made from wood
grown in managed, sustainable forests. It is natural, renewable
and recyclable. The logging and manufacturing processes
conform to the environmental regulations of the country of origin.

Printed in China by C&C.

10 9 8 7 6 5 4 3 2 1

MIX
Paper from
responsible sources
FSC® C008047

Contents

Car safety
Cars are powerful machines. They can be very dangerous.
Always have an adult with you when you look at cars.
Do not stand close to moving cars. Do not walk behind a car.
Make sure the driver can see you.

Cars

You can see cars of all shapes and sizes everywhere you go. Look out for tiny microcars and huge limousines. Listen out for police car sirens and noisy sports car engines.

You can spot amazing cars at racing tracks and museums, too. This book will help you to name the cars you see. It tells you how they work. And it shows you what special features to look out for.

At the back of this book is a Spotter's Guide to help you remember the cars you find. Tick them off as you spot them. You can also find out the meaning of some useful words here.

Turn the page to find out all about cars!

Vintage car

Very old cars are known as vintage cars. They look very different from today's cars. You can spot them in museums, or at vintage car rallies.

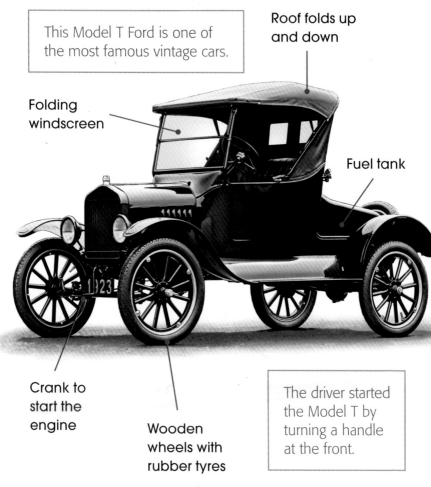

This Model T Ford is one of the most famous vintage cars.

Roof folds up and down

Folding windscreen

Fuel tank

Crank to start the engine

Wooden wheels with rubber tyres

The driver started the Model T by turning a handle at the front.

Microcar

Look out for tiny microcars in cities. Their small size makes them easy to park. They also help to keep city air clean, because they use less fuel than a normal car.

This smart car has plastic body panels that can be recycled.

This car is just 269 cm long

Strong metal frame

Two seats

Luggage compartment

Engine

Plastic body panel

Hatchback

The back end of a hatchback is a large door. This makes it easy to load and unload cargo.

The back seats fold down flat for extra cargo space. This allows the car to carry large things, such as a bike.

Hatch

Removable parcel shelf

Rear seats fold flat for extra storage space

Saloon

A saloon car has separate compartments for people and cargo. Saloons are some of the most popular cars.

Saloons have comfortable seats for at least four people, so they are often used as family cars

Lots of room for rear passengers

Four doors

Separate boot

Engine under bonnet

 # Taxicab

Taxicabs carry passengers on short journeys. Look out for them in towns and cities.

Anyone can hail this London taxi in the street.

Space for five passengers and luggage

Ramp for wheelchairs

Taxis in big cities often look the same as each other. Customers can easily spot them.

Light shows
the taxi is free

A meter measures
how far the taxi
travels. It tells the
driver how much
to charge.

Driver compartment

Estate car

This estate car looks like a stretched saloon! The long boot gives it more space to carry things.

Roof bars allow this car to carry extra cargo on the roof.

High roof over cargo area

Roof bars

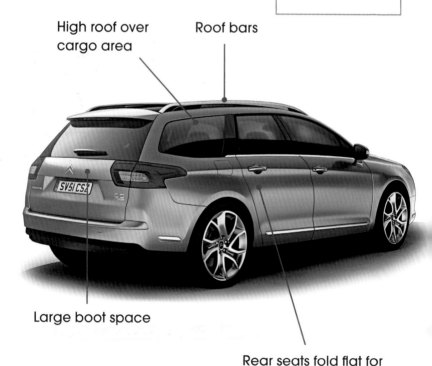

Large boot space

Rear seats fold flat for extra cargo space

People carrier

This people carrier has three rows of seats. This means it can carry more passengers than a normal car can.

Tall roof

Extra row of seats

Large sunroof for a good view

Large boot space

Sliding door

People carriers are popular with large families.

 # Coupe

A passenger car with just two doors is known as a coupe. Some coupes have small back seats. Others have no seats in the back.

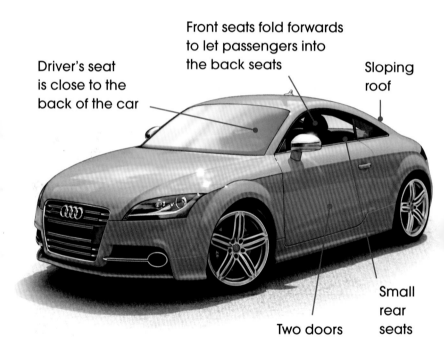

Front seats fold forwards to let passengers into the back seats

Driver's seat is close to the back of the car

Sloping roof

Two doors

Small rear seats

The name coupe comes from a horse-drawn carriage with one row of seats.

Convertible

On a warm day, you might spot a car without a roof. The roof of this convertible folds down into a special space in the boot.

Convertible cars have extra strong chassis to make up for the missing roof.

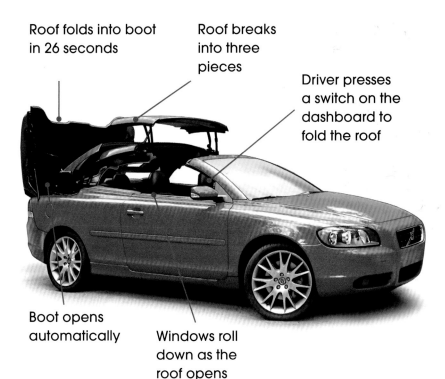

Roof folds into boot in 26 seconds

Roof breaks into three pieces

Driver presses a switch on the dashboard to fold the roof

Boot opens automatically

Windows roll down as the roof opens

Campervan

This campervan is a vehicle by day and a bedroom by night! It is used for camping holidays.

Curtains for privacy at night

Cooker and sink

Bicycle rack

Seats fold down to make a bed

Folding table

When the van is parked, the roof pops up for extra space.

Pop-up roof

This campervan has room for four adults to sleep.

 # Cabriolet

A cabriolet has a folding roof made of tough fabric. They are also known as 'soft tops'.

Roof made of canvas or vinyl

Rear window made of soft plastic

Some cabriolet roofs fold down when the driver presses a button. Others have to be folded by hand.

Sports car

Sports cars are designed to be fast and fun to drive. They have powerful engines and brakes. Most have only two seats. This makes them lighter and faster.

Owners of sports cars can visit a racetrack to drive their car at top speed.

Streamlined
body for speed

Two seats

 # Supercar

If a normal passenger car went as fast as this supercar, it would lift up into the air! Supercars have a special body design that keeps them on the road.

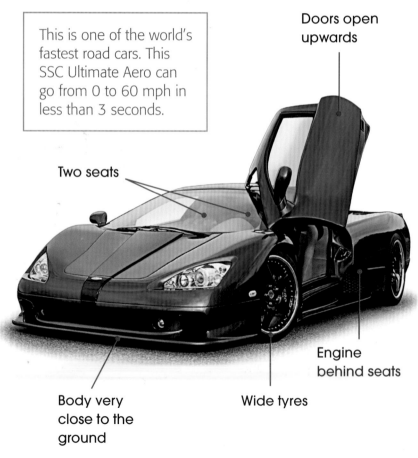

This is one of the world's fastest road cars. This SSC Ultimate Aero can go from 0 to 60 mph in less than 3 seconds.

Doors open upwards

Two seats

Body very close to the ground

Wide tyres

Engine behind seats

Sports Utility Vehicle (SUV)

Sports utility vehicles can be used on and off the road. They can drive through mud, snow, sand and water.

Powerful SUVs can be used to tow trailers, caravans and boats.

Seats are high above the road

Box-shaped body

Body of car high above ground

They are large, with lots of room for people and cargo. This makes them popular with people who live in urban areas, too.

Luxury car

Luxury cars are large and comfortable. You will often spot the owner sitting in the back seat, while a chauffeur does the driving.

Bentleys are famous luxury cars.

Heated leather seats

Long rear overhang

Long bonnet

Mood lighting

Short front overhang

This Bentley is more than five and a half metres long.

DF10 BNN

Classic car

Car makers design new cars every year. But some cars from the past were so popular that people still like to drive them. Some classic cars are very rare. Collectors pay lots of money for them.

This Ferrari Spyder was built more than 50 years ago.

Two seats

Powerful engine

Bumper covered with shiny chrome

Racing car

Some cars are built just for racing. This is a stock car. It looks like the cars that people drive on the road, but don't be fooled.

Sponsors pay for racing cars to be built and raced. Their names are painted on the cars. Stock car racing has many fans in the USA.

Window net to protect the driver in a crash

Sponsor's name

It goes twice as fast as a normal road car. Stock cars race on special oval tracks.

Numbers on the roof and door help the crowd to tell which car is which.

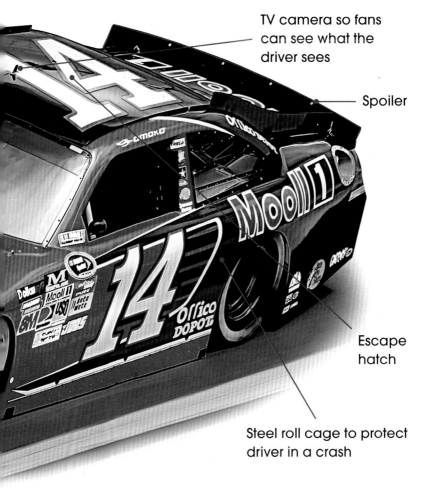

TV camera so fans can see what the driver sees

Spoiler

Escape hatch

Steel roll cage to protect driver in a crash

Police car

The special markings on this car show that there are police officers inside. Police cars drive quickly to emergencies. Flashing lights and a loud siren warn other vehicles. Clear the road!

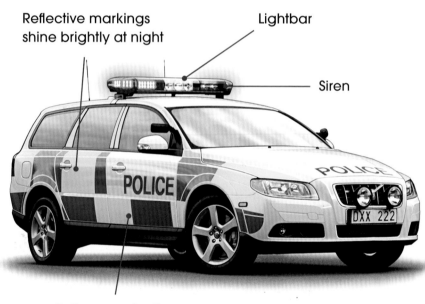

Reflective markings shine brightly at night

Lightbar

Siren

Patterns make the car easy to spot

Police cars have two-way radios so that police officers can talk to each other.

POLICE

POLICE

DXX 222

Electric car

Huge batteries power electric cars. They have to be recharged by plugging the car into an electricity supply. This car takes around 7 hours to recharge.

Electric cars do not produce exhaust fumes. They help to keep the air clean in cities and towns.

Electric motor

Battery under the seats

Charger plug to charge batteries

Solar car

A solar car has an electric motor, but it doesn't need batteries. Special panels on the car turn sunlight into electricity.

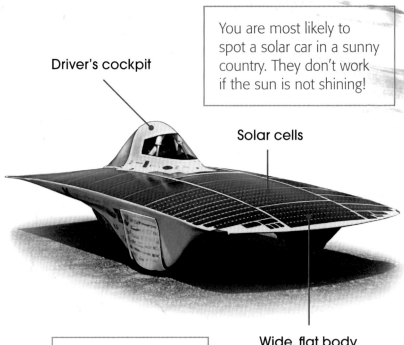

Driver's cockpit

You are most likely to spot a solar car in a sunny country. They don't work if the sun is not shining!

Solar cells

Special solar car races are held in the USA, South Africa and Australia.

Wide, flat body collects as much sunlight energy as possible

Hybrid car

This hybrid car has an electric motor and a petrol engine. The petrol engine does not have to work as hard, so the car uses less fuel.

Using less fuel means fewer exhaust fumes. It also saves money.

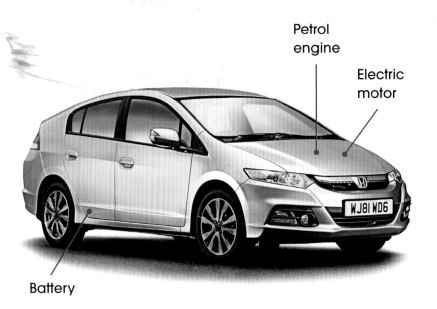

Petrol engine

Electric motor

Battery

Energy is collected when the car brakes, and used to charge the battery.

 # Kit car

You won't see a car like this in a showroom. Kit cars are sold in pieces. The owner has to build their car before they can drive it!

It can take several years to build a kit car.

Some kit cars are designed to look like classic cars

Kit cars have to pass a special test before they can be driven on the road.

Formula One

Formula One racing cars are super fast. Their special shape means they can turn corners at high speed without flying off the road.

The wings on this car work like upside-down aeroplane wings. Instead of lifting the car up, they push it down on to the track.

Rear wing

Wheels outside the car body

Open cockpit

Light body

Front wing

Slick tyres with no treads

Soft rubber tyres get sticky as they heat up, and grip the road

# Armoured car

Armoured vehicles have special features to protect the people inside. This car is called Cadillac One. It is used to transport the US President.

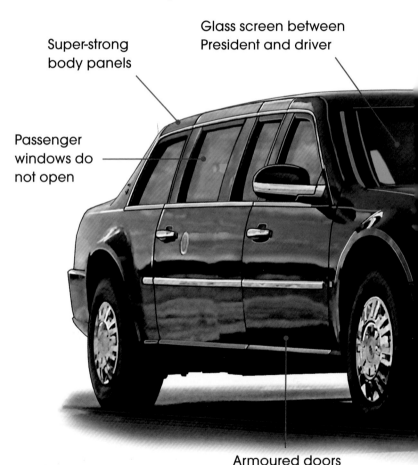

Glass screen between President and driver

Super-strong body panels

Passenger windows do not open

Armoured doors are 20 cm thick

Bottles of the President's blood type are kept on board, in case of an accident or attack.

Specially-trained driver

Bullet-proof glass

Night vision camera

Puncture resistant tyres work even if they are burst

Panel van

This van looks like a passenger car at the front. But the rear is specially adapted to carry things. There is plenty of room for delivering goods, or transporting tools and equipment.

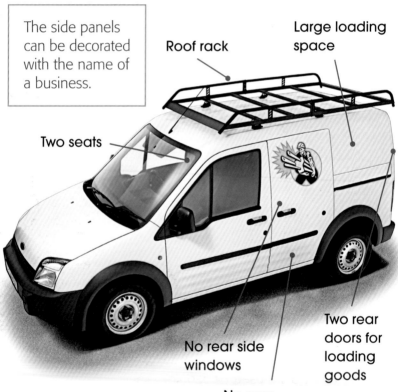

The side panels can be decorated with the name of a business.

Large loading space

Roof rack

Two seats

No rear side windows

No rear passenger seats

Two rear doors for loading goods

Four wheel drive (4x4)

In most cars, the engine only turns two of the wheels. But in a 4x4 vehicle, the engine powers all four wheels. This gives extra control.

It helps off-road vehicles to travel over fields, up mountainsides, and across rivers.

Driver sits high off ground

Strong, tough body

4x4 vehicles are used by people who work in places without good roads, such as farmers.

Large tyres with deep treads

Three-wheeler

At the moment, three-wheelers are rare. But they may become more popular, because they use less fuel than normal cars.

This car has a small engine, like a motorbike.

Room for four people

Luggage space

Teardrop-shaped body

Two back wheels

One front wheel

Some three-wheelers have two wheels at the front and one at the back.

Stretch limousine

A stretch limo is an extra-long luxury car. It has room for many passengers. Limousines often have entertainment and a place to serve drinks. Some even have a hot tub on board!

The biggest stretch limos can carry up to 20 people.

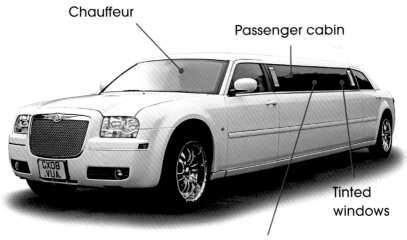

Chauffeur

Passenger cabin

Tinted windows

Passengers sit on long seats around the edges of the cabin

# Dragster

No car speeds up faster than a dragster. These racing cars go from 0 to 100 mph in less than a second! They do this by burning special fuel very quickly.

Before each race, drivers warm the tyres by spinning them. This 'burn out' makes lots of smoke.

Big rear wing

A dragster race lasts for just four seconds.

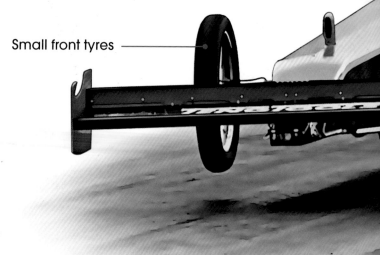

Small front tyres

Parachute to slow down at the end of the race

Engine behind driver

Roll cage to protect driver's head in a crash

Wide rear tyres

Very long chassis made of steel tubes

Driverless car

This car can drive itself! Sensors and cameras collect information about the road ahead. A computer uses this information to drive the car.

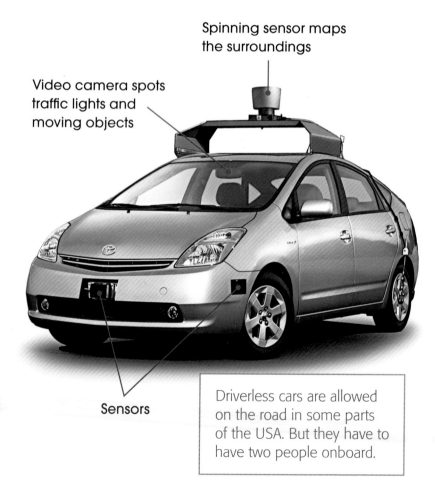

Spinning sensor maps the surroundings

Video camera spots traffic lights and moving objects

Sensors

Driverless cars are allowed on the road in some parts of the USA. But they have to have two people onboard.

Useful words

bonnet a piece of metal that covers a car's engine, and can be opened

boot a space at the back of a car for carrying cargo

chassis the frame that gives a car its shape

engine a machine inside a car, which burns fuel to make the car go

spoiler a small wing-shaped flap stuck on to a car, which helps keep the car on the road when it is driving quickly

tyre the soft rubber that covers car wheels, to help them grip the road

windscreen the glass screen at the front of a vehicle

wing mirror a small mirror on the side of a car, to help the driver see what is behind the car

Spotter's guide

How many of these cars
have you seen? Tick them
when you spot them.

☐ Vintage car
page 6

☐ Microcar
page 7

☐ Hatchback
page 8

☐ Saloon
pages 9

 Taxicab
page 10

 Estate car
page 12

People carrier
page 13

Coupe
page 14

Convertible
page 15

Campervan
page 16

Cabriolet
page 18

Sports car
page 19

Supercar
page 20

Sports Utility
Vehicle (SUV)
page 21

Luxury car
page 22

Classic car
page 23

Racing car
page 24

Police car
page 26

Electric car
page 27

Solar car
page 28

Hybrid car
page 29

Kit car
page 30

 Formula One
page 31

 Armoured car
page 32

 Panel van
page 34

 **Four wheel
drive (4x4)**
page 35

 Three-wheeler
page 36

 **Stretch
limousine**
page 37

 Dragster
page 38

Driverless car
page 40

Find out more

If you would like to find out more about cars, you could visit a motor museum or car rally. These websites are a good place to start.

Haynes International Motor Museum
www.haynesmotormuseum.com

London Motor Museum
www.londonmotormuseum.co.uk

National Motor Museum at Beaulieu
www.beaulieu.co.uk

Heritage Motor Centre, Gaydon
www.heritage-motor-centre.co.uk